The Red Baron
An Ace for the Ages

Shane Simmons

ISBN: 978-1-988954-05-9

Published by Eyestrain Productions
eyestrainproductions.com

"The Red Baron: An Ace for the Ages" cover article and sidebar, "The Baron's Most Famous Mount" originally published in Aviation History, July 1995 and reprinted in Legends of Flight, August 2003, by Cowles History Group; "Dogs of War" originally published in Dog World, August 1995, by Maclean Hunter Publishing; "Laying a Legend to Rest: The Death of the Red Baron" originally written for American Eulogy, 1995.

Table of Contents

The Red Baron:
An Ace for the Ages

IT IS THE MOST romanticized image in air combat history: a
scarlet triplane, piloted by the notorious Red Baron, pluck-
ing another Allied aircraft from the burning French skies of
the Great War, adding it to the long list of kills that made
him the original ace of aces, with 80 confirmed air victories.
The truth about Germany's World War I hero lives up to the
legend, although it took most of the war before this famed
sight became a reality.

Born on May 2, 1892, the eldest of his family's three
sons, Manfred *Freiherr* von Richthofen's career in the military was inevitable. He was enrolled in the military school at
Wahlstatt at age 11, following the wishes of his father, a
Prussian nobleman whose own active military career had
been cut short by deafness. There, he excelled in sports but
fell behind academically, working just enough to get by in
an environment he disliked.

Six years later, Richthofen attended the Royal Military
Academy at Lichterfelde, which he enjoyed more. There he
warmed up to the idea of life in the military and was deter-
mined to apply his riding skills to become a cavalry officer.

After a short time at the Berlin War Academy, he was commissioned as an officer in the 1st Regiment of Uhlans Kaiser Alexander III in April 1911.

The following year he was promoted to *Leutnant*, and was still participating in the regiment horse jumping and racing competitions when World War I broke out in August 1914. Richthofen went into battle with the Uhlans in the early months of the war, and saw action at Verdun. But as static trench warfare set in, the cavalry became obsolete. He served as a messenger during the winter of 1914-15 and was involved in some combat, but he felt there was no glory to be had crawling through muddy trenches and shell holes. Having had his fill of unromantic ground warfare, Richthofen wrote to his commanding general to request a transfer to the air service.

Richthofen knew nothing of flying or air combat and, like many infantrymen, had held aviators in contempt. But now the air offered him a new war, one not restricted by an immobile front line. Richthofen's transfer was approved. Worried that the war would end before he had a chance to do battle in the air, he decided to train as an observer. Pilots were required to undergo three months of training, whereas Richthofen, as an observer, was ready for the field in four weeks.

Sent to Grossenhain on June 10, 1915, Richthofen was the first of his class to be assigned. He began his flying career at *Feldfliegerabteilung* 69 as an observer on the Eastern Front, taking photographs of Russian troop positions. A couple of months later, he transferred to a Western Front unit in Belgium (later to become *Kampfgeschwader* I) as a bombardier.

Richthofen had enjoyed flying from the first moment he took to the air during training. His love of flight was further enhanced by watching the bombs he dropped explode on enemy targets. His fascination with seeing the damage he was inflicting earned him his first war wound. Frantically signalling to his pilot to bank for a clear view after dropping a load on a village near Dunkirk, he accidentally dipped his hand into one of the bomber's propellers and lost the tip of a finger.

In September 1915, Richthofen had his initial tries at air-to-air combat, both times firing on Allied Farman biplanes. The first was an exchange of shots between observers without result. The second encounter ended with the French plane dropping away and crashing after being hit by a couple bursts of machine-gun fire. Richthofen did not receive credit for the victory because the plane had fallen behind enemy lines, robbing him of any physical evidence.

After June 1915, the Fokker Eindekker monoplane series became the most feared aircraft in the sky. Equipped with synchronized machine guns that could fire through the propeller arc without damaging the plane, they gave German scout pilots a firm advantage in air combat. With his new assignment at *Kampfgeschwader* II, Richthofen hoped to get a crack at piloting his own plane. Still flying as an observer, he prevailed upon his friend *Oberleutnant* Georg Zeumer for help. Zeumer was an experienced pilot, and Richthofen had often flown as his observer ever since the two were first teamed on the Eastern Front. After only 24 hours of Zeumer's tutoring, Richthofen took off on his first solo flight, and promptly destroyed his plane while trying to land.

Unwounded and undeterred, Richthofen kept at it, practicing for two weeks before heading off to the flying school at Doberitz. Five months later, he returned to his squadron as a pilot, flying Albatros two-seaters near Verdun. They were not the monoplane scouts he had been hoping for, but once he fixed a gun to the upper wing of his plane, he was able to both fly and take offensive action. April 26, 1916 saw his second kill, a French Nieuport, go down near Fort de Dou-aumont—again behind enemy lines, again not officially counted.

Fokker monoplanes, although successful, were rare at the time. Only Germany's top aces like Max Immelmann and Oswald Boelcke were equipped with those aircraft. When Richthofen finally got a chance to fly a single-seat scout, it was on shared time, with him using it mornings and another pilot flying it afternoons. The Fokker did not give him the success he had expected, and neither pilot did well with their mount. After the second pilot crashed it in no man's land, Richthofen was given another, only to crash that one himself.

Boelcke was Germany's top ace at the time and easily its most respected aviator. Richthofen had met him initially aboard a train while traveling to flying school. The two met again when Richthofen's squadron was returned to the Eastern Front. Boelcke was touring the area in August, assembling pilots for his new *Jagdstaffeln*. Happy, but not wholly content flying bombers and attacking Russian infantry and cavalry with machine-gun fire, Richthofen jumped at Boelcke's offer to join him on the Somme and at last become a full-fledged fighter pilot. He left three days later, and reported for duty back on the Western Front on September 1, 1916.

By then, the monoplanes had lost any advantage they once held. They were now being met in the air by improved Allied scouts also capable of forward firing through the propeller arc. German factories were busy turning out better combat fighters—biplane scouts that featured two front-firing guns. While *Jagdstaffel* 2 awaited delivery of these aircraft for its new fighter pilots, Boelcke trained the men under him in the ways of aerial combat. By the time some Albatros D.II biplanes arrived on the 16th, the pilots were ready for action. The very next day, Richthofen scored his first confirmed kill.

Diving out of the sun with the rest of Boelcke's squadron, on September 17, Richthofen chose an F.E.2b two-seater as his target. His inexperience allowed the Allied observer to get off some dangerous bursts at him, but he finally managed to close in and riddle the belly of the Allied plane. He followed the crippled plane down to the ground. Landing near it, he watched German soldiers lift the two mortally wounded British aviators from their cockpits. The observer, seeing Richthofen and recognizing him as the victor, acknowledged him with a smile before dying. The pilot never regained consciousness and died on the way to hospital.

An avid collector of trophies from the hunt, Richthofen started a personal tradition by ordering a small engraved silver cup to commemorate his victory. He would do the same for the ones that followed soon after. By October 10, he had claimed his place among the German aces with his fifth kill. His victory tally rose at a slow but steady rate, although everything did not always go smoothly. On October 25, he was certain he had recorded his seventh confirmed kill. Much to his displeasure, this victory was contested by two other pilots who claimed the downed B.E.12 as their own. Richthofen insisted there had been no other German planes in the vicinity until after the enemy machine had crashed south of Bapaume. Nevertheless, his claim was disallowed, despite evidence in his favour.

Jasta 2, while distinguishing itself as a top fighter squadron, suffered heavy casualties. Half of its pilots and planes were lost to enemy fire, and other fliers suffered nervous collapse from the strain of battle. Its greatest setback, however, came on October 28. Two days after his 40th victory, Boelcke took to the air with five other planes in his flight.

Richthofen flew at his right wing, Boelcke's friend Erwin Böhme at his left. Details vary as to what happened once they engaged two de Havilland Scouts. Some accounts blame Richthofen's enthusiasm for causing a collision while diving into combat. Others suggest it was Böhme's shaky skills, or merely the confusion of the chase, that sent one plane grinding against the other. What is known for certain is that, for one reason or another, the undercarriage of Böhme's Albatros scraped across Boelcke's upper wing, causing him to lose control of the aircraft. The damaged wing tore away as Boelcke descended, and his plane crashed, crushing his head on impact. Overwhelmed with guilt, Böhme was inconsolable. At Boelcke's grand funeral in Cambrai on the 31st, Richthofen carried his mentor's decorations on a black pillow in the procession.

With Boelcke's death and that of Max Immelmann before him, Germany had lost her top aces. But as Richthofen continued to increase his number of victories, it became apparent that he might fill their shoes. Encouraging him to become Germany's next aviation hero, officials were less strict about confirming his victories, taking him at his word for the few victims that fell behind enemy lines.

One of Richthofen's most famous air battles took place almost a month after Boelcke's death. On November 23, 1916, he went up against Major Lanoe George Hawker, the well-respected commander of No. 24 Squadron, Royal Flying Corps, who had nine air victories and a Victoria Cross to his name. Hawker was in a four-plane flight, led by Captain J.O. Andrews, that attacked five Albatroses south of Bapaume. When the four DH-2s crossed the front lines into German territory, Hawker suddenly found himself alone. Two British planes had had to turn back with engine trouble, and Andrews joined them after being hit and suffering an engine misfire.

Hawker chose his target. As luck would have it, it was Richthofen's Albatros D.II. He dove at the Albatros from behind, getting off a five-round burst that missed when Richthofen cut sharply left. Hawker followed him into the turn. The equally matched pilots began a frantic, spinning chase as each tried to outturn the other and manoeuver into position for a clear shot. Their tight circle, less than 300 feet in diameter, slowly descended from an altitude of almost 10,000 feet to nearly treetop level.

Hawker was now at a disadvantage. Dangerously low on the German side of the lines, he knew he would be hit from the ground or forced to land if he did not end the battle quickly. A succession of loops, which Richthofen's less-creative flying style could not match, placed Hawker in a position to get off another burst that came close, but missed the Baron's plane. Losing his chance, Hawker turned and bolted for his side of the lines with Richthofen in pursuit.

With both the Baron and the ground closing in on him, Hawker zigzagged at high speed to stay out the line of fire. He was nearly saved when Richthofen's first burst jammed his gun. The jam quickly cleared, however, and with his second burst Richthofen shot Hawker through the back of the head. His DH-2 pitched up and then nosed into the ground, just 50 yards short of the German front-line trenches. Richthofen claimed Hawker's Lewis gun from the wreck as a trophy and hung it above the door of his quarters. Hawker was confirmed as Richthofen's 11th victory.

The new year marked a series of successes for Richthofen. With his 16th victory on January 4, 1917, he became the leading living German ace. Along with this latest victory came his reassignment as leader of *Jagdstaffel* 11 at Douai. Two days later, notification came that he was at last to be awarded the *Orden Pour le Mérite*, the "Blue Max," Germany's highest military medal. To further distinguish himself from his fellow fighter pilots, Richthofen started painting sections of his aircraft red, possibly after the colours of his old Uhlan regiment.

Jasta 11, although founded around the same time as *Jasta* 2, held none of the prestige of Richthofen's old squadron, which had come to be known as *Jasta* Boelcke. Since its formation in September 1916, his new unit had not scored a single victory, and it fell upon Richthofen to whip the 12 officers under him into shape. Command did not come easily to him, but he sought to follow in Boelcke's footsteps. Leading by example, he shot down the squadron's first enemy aircraft shortly after his arrival, on January 23, 1917.

Richthofen's red Albatros, now the newer D.III, was already making a name for itself among the Allies. The two-man crew of a British F.E.2b, forced to land as the Baron's 18th victory, referred to "*le petit rouge*" that had brought them down. It was on this same flight that one of the wings of Richthofen's plane cracked, and he had to quickly descend 900 feet for an emergency landing. Another F.E.2b that had fired on him claimed this as a victory, but the wing damage could have been due to structural failure rather than a lucky shot.

With success came fame, and Richthofen's good fortune in combat was milked by the German propaganda machine for all it was worth. Picture postcards and newspaper articles about him circulated widely, and correspondence arrived at his airfield from all over Germany—mostly fan letters from adoring women. The Red Baron had become Germany's number one war hero.

March and April of 1917 saw a thrust of German air power near Arras against Allied forces that outnumbered the Germans by an average of three to one. *Jasta* 11 was in the thick of it, and these two months saw Richthofen bring down another 31 aircraft, surpassing Boelcke's old record. Under his tutelage, the pilots of *Jasta* 11 were fast improving, and competition between them and the fliers of *Jasta* Boelcke was friendly but fierce. Allied fliers began referring to Richthofen's squadron as the "Flying Circus" because of its brightly coloured planes, highlighted in red to match their leader's.

During this period, Richthofen had two close calls. The first occurred shortly after his 25th victory, when enemy fire ruptured his fuel tanks and forced him to shut off his engine, lest it explode, and land near Henin Lietard. April 2 saw another near miss when (according to Richthofen) he was fired upon and hit from the ground by the observer of a Sopwith 1½ Strutter two-seater he had just brought down near Givenchy. In his first report, Richthofen claims to have returned fire and killed the observer, although later he said he held back and did not shoot again despite the dying observer's attack.

The surviving British pilot, however, insisted that his observer was in no condition to fire after their plane hit the ground. Werner Voss, Richthofen's friend and competitor from *Jasta* Boelcke, saw the incident and was cited as a witness to Richthofen's restraint from shooting. The uncertainty of this exchange remains the only blemish on Richthofen's record for chivalry in combat.

By the time Richthofen went on well-deserved leave in May, he had led *Jasta* 11 to more than 100 victories. Lothar von Richthofen, since joining the air service in his brother Manfred's footsteps, had also done well. Within a month of joining up with his brother's squadron, he too had made a name for himself with 20 victories. He was left in charge of *Jasta* 11 while Manfred toured Germany, meeting with the kaiser and other dignitaries, as well as hunting animals and visiting his mother at home in Schweidnitz.

Richthofen returned to the front on June 14 with new orders to organize four *Jagdstaffeln* into a single wing. *Jastas* 4, 6, 10 and 11 became *Jagdgeschwader* I (JG.I). As Richthofen assumed command as *Rittmeister* of JG.I in the Courtrai region, he passed on his command of *Jasta* 11 to *Leutnant* Kurt Wolff.

While leading *Jasta* 11 as their JG.I commander on July 6, Richthofen became involved in an epic dogfight with the British that quickly escalated until there were as many as 40 aircraft in the fray. A chance shot from an F.E.2d, 1,200 feet away, cleaved a two-inch-long groove in Richthofen's skull. He was temporarily paralysed and blinded, and his Albatros fell out of control. Finally regaining the use of his limbs a few thousand feet above the ground, he cut the engine, tore his goggles off, and looked directly at the sun in an effort to clear his vision.

Regaining his sight and realizing he was behind the German lines, Richthofen restarted his engine at 150 feet and searched for a suitable place to set down. Losing his strength and blacking out, he was finally forced to make an emergency landing. The airplane tore down some telephone wires before it came to a rest, and Richthofen tumbled out of his cockpit. He was still conscious when aid came and transported him to St. Nicholas' Hospital in Courtrai.

Despite his nearly fatal wound, Richthofen put himself back on duty at JG.I less than three weeks later, against doctors' recommendations. He was plagued by headaches from the bone fragments still lodged under his scalp and by nausea during flight. But he fought on, all the while insisting Lothar, also wounded in battle, should not return until fully recovered.

The end of August 1917 saw the arrival of the new Fokker F.I triplanes at Courtrai. Richthofen and Voss were among the first to take them into combat. Trading in the

Albatros D.V for what would become his most famous mount, Richthofen shot down his 60th plane, an RE-8, on September 1. It was the last victory he could commemorate with a trophy cup. Silver was becoming scarce in Germany, and Richthofen was forced to discontinue this practice.

The victories he scored on his return to duty failed to inspire Richthofen. After his head wound, he lost much of his zest for combat, and his friends noticed a distinct change in his personality. Already a loner, he became even more withdrawn. Killing was no longer the sport it once had been for him. On September 6, still troubled by his head wound, Richthofen took a period of convalescence to recover more fully. In his absence, his first triplane mount was shot down on September 15, as Kurt Wolff piloted it against a squadron of Sopwith Camels. Voss also met his end in another Fokker F.I during an epic battle on the day of his 48th victory, September 23, outnumbered by a swarm of S.E.5a fighters of No. 56 Squadron led by Major James T.B. McCudden. But Richthofen was back at JG.I on October 23, after visiting home, hunting, recuperating, and finishing writing about air combat in his autobiography.

Richthofen shot down a couple more planes on his return, once again flying an Albatros D.V. He then continued inspecting and testing other aircraft that might fare better than the Fokker triplane—whose safety and suitability in the face of new Allied fighters was already being questioned. Because of official noncombat duties and leave, Richthofen was not able to add to his score again until March 12, 1918, once more flying the Dr.I, as the Fokker Triplane was now designated. Between then and April 20, Richthofen downed his last 16 planes, mostly fighters. The final two victories, Sopwith Camels of No. 3 Squadron, came after the Flying Circus was moved to desolate Cappy.

Richthofen led his flight of triplanes to search for British observation aircraft on the morning of Sunday, April 21, 1918. Four triplanes from *Jasta* 5 were fired on from the ground around 10:30 a.m., after attacking two R.E.8s from No. 3 Squadron, Australian Flying Corps. The antiaircraft fire drew the attention of a flight of Sopwith Camels led by Canadian Royal Air Force pilot Captain Arthur Roy Brown from No. 209 Squadron. Soon after the Camels intercepted and shot down one of the *Jasta* 5 planes, Richthofen's flight joined in the battle.

On the fringe of the fight was Roy Brown's friend, Lieutenant Wilfred R. May, a fellow Canadian. May was a novice pilot, and this was his first offensive patrol. He had been ordered to keep out of combat, but could not resist going after an enemy triplane that passed close by. Jamming his Vickers guns after firing them too long, May headed away from the battle toward the Somme Valley, defenceless.

Richthofen, from above, spotted the lone plane breaking off and chose it for his next victim. Brown, seeing this chase unfolding a few thousand feet below him, dove to help his fellow airman. He realized that the lone Camel stood little chance with the red triplane hot on its tail. May, panicking and losing altitude, tried every wild manoeuver he could think of to stay out of the Baron's sights. It was only the unpredictability of the inexperienced pilot's moves that kept Richthofen from picking him off quickly with his probing shots.

"Richthofen was giving me burst after burst from his Spandau machine guns. The only thing that saved me was my awful flying. I didn't know what I was doing," May would say later.

It was then, with Brown closing from behind, that Richthofen, usually a meticulous and disciplined fighter pilot, made a mistake and broke one of his own rules by following

May too long, too far and too low into enemy territory. Two miles behind the Allied lines, as Brown caught up with Richthofen and fired, the chase passed over the machine-gun nests of the 53rd Battery, Australian Field Artillery. Sergeant C.D. Popkin opened fire with his Vickers, followed by Gunners William Evans and Robert Buie, plus a number of riflemen.

Richthofen was hit, but the debate over who fired the shot that passed through his torso, killing him, goes on. None of the principal shooters ever said with certainty that he was the one who got him. Those who defended the shooters' claims were their friends and colleagues, choosing sides based more on nationality and emotion than hard evidence.

Top Canadian ace Billy Bishop is one who supported his countryman, saying, "Nobody will ever convince anyone who flew in World War I that anyone but Roy Brown shot down Richthofen." He also suggested a bias against Canadian flyers, "Had he been in any other air force he would have been given credit and would probably have received half a dozen decorations from his own and other countries."

Whether hit from the air or the ground, Richthofen was mortally wounded. He tore off his goggles, opened the throttle briefly, then cut off the engine and dipped down for a crash landing. His plane bounced once, breaking the propeller, and settled in a beet field alongside the Bray-Corbie road near Sailley-le-Sac. He died moments later. It was 10:50 a.m.

Manfred Von Richthofen was laid to rest late on the afternoon of April 22 in a small, unkempt cemetery in Bertangles. He was buried with full military honours after a short service by an Anglican chaplain. Twelve men from No. 3 Squadron, Australian Flying Corps, each fired three rounds into the air. Other officers placed wreaths on the grave. The body was set with feet facing the marker, a four-

bladed propeller trimmed to form a cross. Upset about a
German being buried in their cemetery, the villagers descended on the grave that night, uprooted the marker and
tried to dig up the body.

That same evening, RAF pilots dropped canisters containing news of Richthofen's death and pictures of his
funeral over *Jagdgeschwader* I, confirming the fears of the
German officers there. *Oberleutnant* Wilhelm Reinhard
succeeded Richthofen as commander of JG.I, as per Richthofen's wishes, but he only lasted two months; *Oberleutnant*
Hermann Wilhelm Göring assumed command after Reinhard's death.

Richthofen's body was moved after the war to a larger
cemetery at Fricourt. His brother, Karl Bolko, had his body
moved again in 1925, this time to Berlin where, in a large
state funeral with thousands in the procession, he was buried
at Invaliden Cemetery. A modest flat memorial stone was
unveiled the following year by his mother. Göring added a
monument in 1938. All the Red Baron's war trophies, an
impressive collection kept at his home, were lost when the
Russians advanced through Schweidnitz near the end of
World War II.

Manfred von Richthofen died in battle nearly a century
ago, but the legend of the Red Baron still retains its fascination. There was much regret from both sides that he did not
survive the war. But his death, as much as his life, assured
his continued presence in history as one of World War I's
greatest enigmas.

The Baron's Most Famous Mount

MANFRED VON RICHTHOFEN spent most of World War I flying Albatros biplanes, but he is still most readily associated with the Fokker Dr.I triplane that he made famous.

The tendency of the Albatros D.III's single-spar lower wing to break off in flight had nearly cost Richthofen his life on January 24, 1917. When it happened again, on April 8, to one of his subordinates, Richthofen was inspired to write a harsh letter to the engineering department in Berlin. He also outlined his specific criticisms of the D.III and enumerated the qualities that made for a good fighter scout.

That month, Dutch designer Anthony Fokker, noted for his aircraft designs for the German war machine and for his development of the interrupter gear for synchronized forward-firing machine guns, visited Richthofen at *Jasta* 11. Together they went out to the trenches to watch the British Sopwith Triplane in action. It was believed that three wings gave an airplane more manoeuvrability and greater climbing speed. Richthofen wanted a comparable design.

Technical reports from captured Sopwiths were unavailable at the time, but Fokker went ahead anyway, modifying one of his biplane designs into a triplane, which he initially designated the Fokker V.3. The production order was granted on July 14, and the F.I, as it was now called, passed its acceptance tests on August 16. Richthofen had the first two combat-ready planes at *Jagdgeschwader* I on the 21st. Later, improved production triplanes were redesignated Fokker Dr.Is.

Slow but nimble, the Fokker Dr.I was the climber that Richthofen had wanted, able to reach 13,000 feet in just 11 minutes. Nineteen feet long, nine feet high, with its top wing spanning 23 feet, seven inches, it was a small plane. Twin Spandau machine guns, controlled by two separate buttons on the control stick, fired over a nose that many said resembled a face. The Fokker Dr.I, however, was 35 mph slower than the Spad 13, and was even outrun by some British bombers, such as the de Havilland DH-4.

Two incidents of the Dr.I's losing its top wing at the end of October grounded it until a strengthened wing cleared it for use again a month later. Other lesser incidents in the early months of 1918 shed further doubt on the structural integrity of the plane, but poor quality control proved to be the problem. After a government crackdown on Fokker, the reliability of his Dr.Is improved.

Other German aces who distinguished themselves in the Dr.I, included Erich Löewenhardt, Lothar von Richthofen, Werner Voss, Ernst Udet, and Josef Jacobs. But it was Manfred von Richthofen, despite flying the plane for a total of only six weeks, who forever made it his own. He flew five different Dr.Is in combat, all of them marked in red, but only one that was totally red. Nineteen of his 80 victories were scored in the Fokker. Richthofen died in a Dr.I while pursuing what would have been another win for himself and the triplane.

Never widely used by other airmen, and quickly outdated, the Fokker Dr.I nevertheless proved itself the mount of choice for some of Germany's top fliers—men whose skills could overcome the plane's shortcomings and use its better qualities to full advantage.

Dogs of War

THE BARON DIVES, intent on his kill, his twin Spandau machine guns blazing. The red triplane roars past the World War I flying ace, crippling his mount in the deadly strafing. The doghouse, riddled with bullets and coughing dense clouds of black smoke, noses down for a crash landing. Snoopy, the pilot, raises a clenched fist and curses out the Red Baron, swearing to meet him in aerial combat again.

That, at least, is how in happens in the panels of "Peanuts" on the funny pages. The reality was a little different.

The Red Baron, Manfred *Freiherr* von Richthofen, was the most famous air ace of the first world war. His scarlet biplane (later a Fokker triplane) was the last sight many Allied pilots saw before they went down in flames over the western front. He's credited with bringing down an unequalled 80 aircraft, although his actual total is at least three planes higher. He was a chivalrous killer, respected on both sides of the front for his skill and bravery under fire as he led his squadron, Richthofen's Flying Circus, to victory after victory.

Charlie Brown's imaginative pet Beagle never entered the picture. But there was another dog in the Baron's life—one that played the role of constant friend and companion.

While on leave in Ostend with one of his fellow pilots, Georg Zeumer, the Baron met up with a Belgian man who was anxious to sell off the puppies from a litter of purebred Great Danes. The aces purchased two of the pups for five marks each. Zeumer named his dog "Max"; the Baron chose the name "Moritz" for his own.

Richthofen came from a family of nobles. Like many nobles, he enjoyed hunting for sport. He had kept hunting dogs before, but there was no call for them on the front, where his sport had become Allied airmen instead of woodland beasts. After years at war, being highly regarded in the public eye but distant and something of a loner, he at last found regular companionship and friendship with Moritz.

Moritz grew at a startling rate. On hind legs he stood nearly as tall as his master. His size prompted the Baron to jokingly refer to him as his "lap dog." The two accompanied each other to different assignments and lived in close company. Moritz would always be waiting on the airfield for Richthofen's return when the killing for the day was done. Despite the dog's enormous size, he shared the Baron's modest bed every night, ready to see him off on a dawn patrol at a moment's notice.

Moritz wasn't the only pilot's dog to crowd his master's bed, however. Richthofen's frequent adversary, Canadian ace Billy Bishop, who was stationed across the front from him for part of the war, had a similar arrangement. Bishop went up against the Flying Circus on a number of occasions. After a long day of dogfighting he would return to the west side of the front for another dogfight – this one for bedding space. One of his dogs was a large black hound that he allowed into bed with him on bad nights, despite being quoted as calling him "quite the smelliest dog I have ever known."

A dog's life at an aerodrome, either Allied or German, could be comfortable. The pilots were keen to have canine companions about, and even the mangiest of mutts found plenty of food and affection. The unclaimed stragglers could always rely on some aviator, gunner or mechanic to find them a bowl of rations and give them a scratch behind the ears. In return, the dogs would help keep the tents clear of vermin. "Ratting" was a popular canine game.

Despite the dogs' carefree lives, they were still caught up in the gears of mechanized warfare like everyone else on and near the front. There were many dangers at the aerodrome. Moritz's brother Max, whose life ended under the wheels of a car, was one of the unlucky ones. His master, Zeumer, was killed in combat soon after.

Chasing planes was the favourite pastime for many aerodrome dogs, and Moritz was no exception. Although it was great fun for the dogs, it was even more treacherous than running after cars. Many dogs were killed when they got too close to the spinning propellers, and Moritz had a narrow escape from one of them. He was struck by a plane he caught up with, which sliced cleanly through his ear. He howled terribly and, as the Baron put it, "a very beautiful propeller was ruined."

Richthofen had never bothered to get Moritz's ears clipped to stand upright. He considered it the one failing in his training. But after the accident, when the bandages came off, Moritz was left with one ear standing half upright and one floppy. Forever after he looked rather lopsided. It didn't bother the dog, but his master thought Moritz would be quite handsome if not for this lone defect.

It was the Sunday morning of April 21, 1918 when Manfred von Richthofen took off on his final patrol. As always, Moritz was there to faithfully see him into the air and await his return. His master never came back. While flying low over an Australian-held sector of the front, in pursuit of what would have been his 81st confirmed air victory, he was shot through the back, either by the pilot of a Sopwith Camel that had joined the chase or by one of the gunners of the ground forces. Richthofen crash landed near the ruins of Sailley-le-Sac and died moments later when the bullet entered his heart. A legend was dead at age 25.

What happened to Moritz after that is a mystery, but it's fair to speculate he was waiting for his master on the airfield of Richthofen's command when news of his death came a day later. A Royal Air Force flight dropped a canister over the base at Cappy with a brief message: "Rittmeister von Richthofen was fatally wounded in aerial combat and was buried with full military honours."

A hero of the Great War was gone, survived by his parents, his sister, his two brothers and a dog that had served to show a compassionate, tender side to the most feared man in the French skies. Between accounts of air victories and discussion of air combat strategy, Richthofen took time to note in his personal journal, "The most beautiful creature ever created is my elm-coloured Great Dane, my 'little lap dog,' Moritz."

Laying a Legend to Rest:
The Death of the Red Baron

RACING OVER THE Allied trenches in his scarlet triplane, hot on the tail of what would have been his 81st confirmed kill, fate caught up with the Red Baron in the form of a single bullet. At age 25, on the morning of April 21, 1918, the highest scoring ace of the first world war was shot through the back, either by a pursuing Sopwith Camel pilot or the Australian ground troops. After years as a fighter pilot, earning himself a reputation as the most feared man in the French skies, Manfred von Richthofen was no longer a living legend.

As one of the most famous heroes of World War I, a career soldier and nobleman, Richthofen was guaranteed a lavish military funeral. Unfortunately, he was one of the few German aces to be shot down on the Allied side of the front, so it fell upon the British to bury one of their greatest enemies.

The funeral they arranged the next day was official and polite. Richthofen's body was driven to a small unkempt cemetery in Bertangles, not far from where he met his end. There, officers laid wreathes on the grave, an Anglican chaplain gave a brief service, and twelve rifles were fired three times in salute by the No. 3 Squadron Australian Flying Corps. The body, probably by accident, was set to rest with the feet facing a cross that had been crafted from a four-bladed airplane propeller. The plaque on the marker incorrectly listed his age as 22.

That night, local villagers, angered that a German had been buried in their cemetery, descended on the grave, destroyed the flowers, overturned the marker, and tried to dig up the Baron. They did not share the respect most Allied soldiers and pilots felt towards their chivalrous opponent.

While Richthofen's grave was being desecrated in Bertangles, RAF pilots crossed the front to inform the Germans of their loss. Canisters were dropped over enemy aerodromes, each containing a message that ran, "Rittmeister von Richthofen was fatally wounded in aerial combat and was buried with full military honours." Pictures of the funeral accompanied the sad news.

Following the war, Richthofen's remains were moved to a much larger cemetery at Fricourt, and then again, in 1925, to Invaliden Cemetery in Berlin. At last he got his grand funeral, with thousands of patriotic Germans joining the procession. The state service was held on November 20 and was attended by British and American dignitaries. Richthofen's mother, his youngest brother, and Field Marshal von Hindenburg led the rest of the Richthofen family and the surviving members of his old command to the grave site that was to be his final resting place.

Richthofen's mother unveiled a flat memorial stone the following year. In 1938, Hermann Göring, who had inherited Richthofen's command shortly after his death, had a monument built around the grave.

History remembers Manfred von Richthofen, the Red Baron, as a romantic knightly figure, reserved and private— an enigma to all who knew and flew with him. But, as grand a hero as he was to his own countrymen, he was remembered just as fondly by those he fought long and hard against. As a British aviation journal of the time wrote in a respectful obituary, "He was a brave man, a clean fighter and an aristocrat. May he rest in peace."

Bibliography

BAKER, David. *Manfred von Richthofen: The Man and the Aircraft He Flew*. The Outline Press, 1990

BISHOP, William Avery. *Winged Warfare*. Pan Books, Ltd., 1967

SHORES, Christopher. *Air Aces*. Presidio Press, 1983

JOHNSON, J.E. *Full Circle: The Story of Air Fighting*. Chatto & Windus Ltd., 1964 - also: revised and enlarged edition. *The Story of Air Fighting*. Arrow Books Limited, 1985

LONGSTREET, Stephen. *The Canvas Falcons: The Story of the Men and Planes of World War I*. The World Publishing Company, 1970

MELADY, John. *Pilots: Canadian Stories from the Cockpit - From First Flight to the Jet Age*. McClelland & Stewart Inc., 1989

RICHTHOFEN, Manfred Freiherr von. *The Red Baron: An Autobiography of the Most Famous Air Ace of WWI, the Famed Red Knight of Germany*. Folkestone & Bailey, 1974

ROWE, R.P.P. *A Concise Chronicle of Events of the Great War*. Philip Allan and Co., 1920

STOKESBURY, James L. *A Short History of Air Power*. William Morrow and Company, Inc., 1986

TAYLOR, John W.R. & MUNSON, Kenneth (editors). *History of Aviation: Military Air Power*. New English Library, 1975

About the Author

Shane Simmons is an award-winning screenwriter and graphic novelist whose work has appeared in international film festivals, museums and lectures about design and structure. His art has been discussed in multiple books and academic journals about sequential storytelling, and his short stories have been printed in critically praised anthologies of history, crime and horror. He lives in Montreal with his wife and too many cats.

Also by Shane Simmons

Novels

Necropolis
Sex Tape
Filmography

Booklets

Carrion Luggage
Hot Pennies
Choke the Chicken

Graphic Novels

The Long and Unlearned Life of Roland Gethers
The Failed Promise of Bradley Gethers
The Inauspicious Adventures of Filson Gethers

Last Words

Small-press publishers rely on reviews from readers like you to help get the word out about their books. Whether it's a simple star rating or a written critique, every bit of feedback helps convince the impersonal computer algorithms of Amazon, and other literary outlets, that the book you just read has merit and deserves more exposure. Please support independent authors, editors and publishers by taking a few moments to share your thoughts and opinions with other potential readers who may be sitting on the fence about trying an intriguing novel or collection. Your suggestions or comments can make all the difference when it comes to helping them find a new writer they'll like, or matching a struggling author with the readership he or she deserves. Thank you.

www.ingramcontent.com/pod-product-compliance
Lightning Source LLC
Chambersburg PA
CBHW071800020426
42331CB00008B/2346